WE ALL MAKE IT OUT IN THE END

Lacey Roop

Write About Now Publishing

2023

WE ALL MAKE IT OUT IN THE END

Editor: C.L. "Rooster" Martinez
Editor-in-Chief & Typesetting: M.R. "Chibbi" Orduña
Associate Editor: Amir Safi
Cover Design: Morgan Williams

Published by:
Write About Now Publishing, Texas, USA
www.wanpoetry.com | @wanpoetry

Library of Congress Control Number:
Print ISBN: 978-0-9906127-2-8
Ebook ISBN: 978-0-9906127-3-5
Printed in USA

If you are viewing this publication as an ebook, so that you may experience this book as it was intended, the publishers recommend you scale your font so that the text below appears on one complete line.
This line is a size guide; change the font size in your ebook reader so the text fits in one line only.

WWW.WANPOETRY.COM | @WANPOETRY

For anyone who has ever felt othered.

& to family— the chosen & the ones we come from.

You don't drown by falling in the water;

you drown by staying there.

— Ed Cole

In the end, what matters is this: I survived.

— Gail Honeyman

BUCKTOOTHED & BELONGING

I grew up bucktoothed & awkward.
A loudmouthed whippersnapper with a drawl
        that dragged like brakes on gravel

underneath a honeyed sun.
        Every time my hometown said,
ain't no girl can play ball as good as a boy

        I took pride in sending home
their sons with black eyes & broken egos.
        I made all their daughters laugh & cheer

in a way that made the town a little weary.
        Sleepover invitations never came
'cuz no one knew which bedroom I belonged in.

        My small town felt more
like a closed closet than an open door.
        I was raised in a place known as the hospitality state,

yet didn't feel welcomed—
        like I was born misplaced.
Little lemon,

        couldn't even bleed right.
Always felt odd.
        So one night I decided to

pull out an atlas
        & rip out a map of the United States–
closed my eyes & threw a dart

        that landed in a little blue spot
located in the largest red state.
        & when I arrived,

I woke up for the first time
        in a place that finally didn't feel like
drowning.

        I stumbled into an open mic
& found other people that couldn't be placed
        neatly into boxes either.

Heard the word *Queer*–
        wore it like a badge of honor,
found my tribe in

        those not ashamed
to live their most
        authentic lives.

O Austin,
Kingdom of *The Heavenly Odd & Awkward.*

Palace of *We Got All the Queer Kids' Backs.*
Temple of *Come As You Are & Be Loud & Proud About it.*

To every small town weirdo,
to every person shamed for being uniquely you,

a birthplace is just that— a place where you were born,
but home is where you get to choose who you become.

You belong; you always have.
I am so glad you made it–

Wherever you are.
Welcome home.

BLOOD COUSIN

Sam says if you swallow a tablespoon of local honey you won't get sick with allergies. He says swallow it down with a cup of faucet water; no ice. Sam says sunscreen was invented just for people who don't like to get their hands dirty. Sam's never been out of Mississippi. Sam says school is for suckers which is why he dropped out when he was 15. He says when a tornado comes you best be in a bathtub or in a doorway. Sam says he can fix anything by hand— blindfolded. I believe him. My second cousin from a long line of southern sweatworkers & backbreakers. You can tell the lineage of a man by the size of his hands & Sam's hands are Texas grapefruits; red, slightly bruised with pink around the edges— fingernails stained in grease. They are full of juice & blood & hot sweat. Callused as tough as leather stretched around each knuckle like a stubborn tarp. What Sam won't say is that he sniffs every flower like the finest perfume. Makes the prettiest defense about it. Says his nose is so sharp he can smell where the bees have eaten… & fucked. I tell Sam, *nobody knows what you know,* & we both laugh at the ambiguity of what that means. Sam doesn't comment like the other guys do about my boy jeans; he just says, *I think we are wearing the same pair. They fit you alright?* & I know what he means. Sam once beat a grown man's jaw into the pulp of the earth without ever breaking a sweat just because the man made a comment about what he would do to me once I went through puberty. Through curdled blood the man fumbled through the hole in his lip & said, *I'll kill you, son.* Sam handed him his own gun & said, *You kill me & I'll haunt you so bad your own ghost will shoot itself.* Sam & I never spoke about that incident because I didn't know whether to thank him or hit him for almost getting himself locked up or shot over something as dumb as that. Sam tells me, *I love you just the way you are, cousin.* Sam says, *if anyone does you wrong I'll break every knuckle, I'll bite off their tongue.*

BDE

He stares at me as if I'm something
to be beaten, prized, or shamed.

By the question mark in his eyebrows
I can't tell if he'd rather hunt me
like a deer
just to hang on his wall,
or shoot me &
let the vultures do what they want
with my body.

I stare back.

I notice his mouth is more bullwhip than bite
& I was born with four sets of teeth, *brah*.
Ain't afraid to rip through the flesh & spit out the bone
if that is what it takes to save
my body.

Over a pint of beer I poured him
he finally leans over the bar top & asks,
So... what are you, anyway?

Knowing what he meant
I haphazardly reply,
Genderbender.

To which he responds,
So you are like.... magic?

Out of all the people on this planet
I had no idea that this guy would be
the one to say one of the most illuminating
things to me.

Yes! I exclaim. *You are correct; my gender is magic.*
The body & all its perplexities— praiseworthy.
Miraculous be the reclamation
& resurrection of self. To be so comfortable in your own skin
that you claim your shadow, too.
Wear it like lipstick or a suit, or a little of both.

Don't apologize for the way your body moves,
for how alive your hips feel in the clothes
you were taught not to wear.

Did you know that clownfish can change their genders too?

Hawkfish are bi-directional,
meaning they can switch their sex
as many times as they like.

Male seahorses get pregnant.

& with hyenas,
not only are the females the fierce leaders of the pack,
but their clitorises are also larger than erect
male penises.

How cool is that?!

That we all exist in the same wild kingdom.
How we all possess a body riddled with magic.

I don't know why some have a hard time understanding
how necessary & natural shapeshifting is for some of us.

How it has never been about hiding a body,
but unearthing one.

How I am more boy than man & no woman at all.

That just because I have a vagina
doesn't mean my balls aren't huge.

This body is mine
in the same way that your body is yours.

& if that is a threat to you, sir,
then I guess you should grow a pair.

BOYS WILL BE BOYS

The television is a lit sparkler in the living room
that us kids congregate around as we fight over the control.
The boys win because when Ashley gripped the remote tight,
Thomas held her wrist even tighter, pulled it to the floor,
& farted loudly into her forearm– she dropped it instantly.
The boys hooted & hollered in victory & then argued
over whether to watch *Ren & Stimpy* or *Mortal Kombat*.
Us girls didn't speak up because even though we were all
in the same room, we knew we didn't sit at the same table.
Our girl voices more echo than origin.

Laura, aimless & bored with the flicking of stations,
found a basket of barbies.
She invites us girls to play too. We give them names
& favorite colors & dream vacations & careers & ages
& let them pick the restaurant of their choosing. The boys,
now curious about our disappearance, decide to find us.
Their eyes switchblade open at the sight & invite themselves in.
Jane says, *Get out stupids*,
as Seth lunges forward & rips
a barbie that Jane had named Margaret
from her hands.
He glances over his shoulder
to the other boys & says, *Look at this*,
as he slides the plastic woman's shirt over her chest.
Oooh la la, they screech as they come closer.
Kari pushes Mark away,   *Stop it! Get out!*
as Kevin picks up another
barbie, who I had just given a promotion,
named Desiree.
Look at this one! He smirks while pulling at her skirt.

Us girls' voices get louder—
we crescendo & crash & plead.
Stop. No. This isn't funny. Get out. Get Out! Stop!!
I said *No. NO!!! Stop!*

Please.

& on the last word
they pause—

look at us, smirk & say,
All you had to do was ask nicely.

What they leave in their boy wake is not a basket of barbies anymore,
but a casket of women—
some plastic & others
barely girls.

HEIDI EXPLAINS BLOWJOBS
AT A GIRLS' SLEEPOVER

We are huddled in the kitchen getting our fourth can of soda
when Heidi notices a bowl of Blow Pops on the counter.
She asks Whitney if she has ever sucked her boyfriend's dick.
Whitney instantly turns into a turtle.
Her face now chagrin red, she shakes her head, *No*, fast
as it recedes into her neck & says, *Never! We are just in the 7th grade!*
We all giggle as Heidi pulls the wrapper off a blue Blow Pop
& says, *y'all need to learn how since we will be in 8th grade soon.*
Carrie, who won't even hold hands with a boy,
looks like she just swallowed a ghost pepper.
Mortified, she exclaims, *Oh my gosh, Heidi! You've done that?*
Heidi begins to move the sucker toward her mouth
as she speaks so matter-of-factly with a smirk
that seems as if she is relishing in our shock.
He is older & on the baseball team &
likes it in the car after a game.

We watch as if we are watching a scary movie–
hands over our faces with eyes peeking through our young fingers
as Heidi moves the Blow Pop in & out of her child mouth.
She doesn't do it for long because she says it doesn't take long,
but her mouth is now stained blue
like the saddest bruise.

The other girls have lots
of questions because Heidi with the blue mouth has now
become the official 7th grade sex guru based off how
well she can please a Blow Pop.

I look at them all
& think how easy it is going to be for a boy with careless hands
to unwrap & stain them.
How sweet girls can be like that—
suckers.

Thirteen & already thinking about
the pleasure of another over their own.

The quickness of youth gone
as easily as a candy eaten.

LACEY EXPLAINS SELF-LOVE
AT A GIRLS' SLEEPOVER

Suppressing my
timidity for a moment, I mutter,
but have any of you touched yourselves to see what you like?

& maybe that
was the moment people suspected
I was a lesbian or weird or creepy.

No one looked shocked or embarrassed as much as scared & ashamed—
as if their bodies were the enemy all along.

We finish our sodas, grab another
before heading upstairs to watch a movie.
Our sleeping bags all splayed next to one another.

When the lights turned off, Susan Ashley– perhaps the most beautiful
& popular of us all–
put her lips to my ear &
whispered, *I like that you're different.*

PURPLE COAT

I was not like other girls—
        especially in Mississippi.

        I grew up crooked,
& dressed like my father.

        Anyone who told me girls
couldn't wear high-tops or button-ups,

        I punched them.
My mom thought more church would help me *straighten*

        up, but I've always been better
                at *bending*.

It wasn't until 8th grade
        when I first learned about gender & sexuality.

It was from my psychology teacher who taught us,
        Lesbianism is a mental disorder that derives from penis envy.

I assured her that wasn't true since
        I had the biggest dick

in all of middle school.
        In high school,

        I remember a boy named Drew Henry.
He wore a purple coat.

I envied how brave he was to wear it.
        How he stared down the throats

of so many people who attached faggot to his name
        & how I was too afraid to say anything

because I didn't want to be outed.
        It is a shame how so many kids are taught

        to hide their hearts
& condemn their skin.

The fact that homosexuality exists in 1500 species
& homophobia exists in 1

is proof that love is something
human beings need more of.

To all the boys in purple coats–

to the tough girls
& gay soldiers–

to the long haired dudes
& the buzz cut dykes–

to the genderqueers, trans, bi & straight allies–

your heart is the holiest chapel.
Love the sharpest sword.
Your skin is a carefully stitched miracle;
I hear that even God marvels
at how it fits you
so well.

It would be absurd if we did not understand both angels and devils, since we invented them.

— John Steinbeck

Home / is it shelter or capture?

HOMEWARD BOUND

My father shot my dog

       in front of me

to teach him

       a lesson about

not digging out—

       not trying to leave

the family.

       My father loved that dog

probably more

       than I did.

He cried & cried & cried at his death.

       I cried, too.

Looking back on it now,

       I think I cried the most

seeing my dad sad.

       Recognizing my father was human

just like everyone else.

       But also witnessing what my father

was capable of doing, if anyone,

       including the dog,

tried to leave.

HELON

The first time I saw blood

coming out of a body

I was five.

It was my brother's blood.

We were at a playground

covered in rocks.

He was a swinging bundle of limbs.

His body—

a fat little watermelon;

his insides the same color red.

I saw him burst

the moment he let go

of the swing.

The shell of him

split at the chin.

The liquid the most radiant color

of hurt.

My parents looked appalled—

angry at the mess

of each other.

I watched, helpless as a dead deer

as my parents screamed & screamed

while my brother quietly wept

& bled.

BEFORE THE BEGINNING

I awoke to find the world had tilted.

Even my feet switched places—
my right foot now on my left.

The coffee pot was full of flowers,
roses with thorns & stems.

I know this because one pricked
me on the sip down.

I coughed up blood
the color of a peach.

It tasted not of iron,
but of a memory

I thought I had forgotten,
which was me on a swing

in a park with legs not long enough
to touch the ground,

with a mom & a dad laughing & in love
& happy in a moment that would not last forever—

when we were all so young & still together,
before the world split

& we all fell apart.

A STONE'S THROW AWAY

Superman was small fries compared to my SUPERDAD!

He could carry the entire neighborhood on his shoulders—

throw us from one end of the pool to the other

with such ferocity

we were known in the neighborhood

as the *Flying Kids.*

Until one day my father threw us so far

we all woke up twenty-two years later.

When we saw each other again

we could barely recognize our faces.

We had to ask,

I'm sorry, who are you again?

KILLER WHALES

I'm reading about orcas & their families
& I'm thinking about how me & my family have nothing in common with orcas.
I'm thinking about how my parents
were married for twenty years,
but how the marriage was tumultuous–
riddled with hornets' nests,
& how the divorce went badly & how
my brother didn't talk to my dad for
almost twenty years & how I moved away
to Texas & how just yesterday
my dad disowned me via a text message,
but I'm also thinking about the time we all
went to Disney World & how everything
was supposed to be magical, but it wasn't,
& I'm thinking about how our Christmas mornings looked as perfect as a postcard–
the way presents would engulf the entire living room,
but how it still felt empty, like something was missing
& I'm thinking about
how my dad was an awesome coach,
but couldn't leave his yelling on the field
& how my mom was a terrible cook,
but she was also the one who taught me how to swim
& I'm thinking that I am thirty
& that once upon a time my parents were thirty,
but they had one kid named Lacey who was four
& another named Helon who was two &
they all lived in a small town called Tupelo, MS
in a brick house on 1806 Bob White Drive
& how I was a just child
with a baby brother
& how I had a mom & a dad
& we were all so new to this—
to each other really.
& I'm thinking about my mom pulling my first tooth
& my dad bringing home a puppy
& how bright & full of love & right
everything was until it wasn't
& no one knows what happened
or why,

but something
did collapse
& when it did there was no home.
Just a house. There was no son or daughter or
dad or wife, just four people with the same
last name. We had hands,
but no touch.
Mouths,
but no words.
& I'm thinking
I don't know what it means to be a parent—
I'm thinking, would I ever regret my children, too?
& now I'm reading about orcas again
about how they never abandon a family
member even if they become sick or old or disabled
& I'm thinking my parents are in their sixties
& the average American lifespan is seventy-eight
& I'm thinking how do the orcas fucking do it?
How do they stay a family forever?
Even when an orca dies,
every member bands together to hold the corpse
& if the body is small enough,
the female will put her loved one in her mouth
& carry them
wherever she goes.

THE WEDDING

My parents fought my entire life.
Twenty years of screaming—
            even on the holidays.

The house a permanent
            carousel of chaos.
The two of them—

            acrobats of arguing.
The wedding
            had to have been a happy day

for them, but the marriage a mistake
            my brother & I got to witness.
I have learned of love as a thing

            that wilts—never blooms,
but I have always been defiant.
            There are certain things that

I cannot believe are true.
                        I have a recurring dream that
if my parents were to meet again

            my limbs would fall off.
In one week I will marry the one I love
            & they both ask if one parent can come,

but not the other.
            I tell them about my dream.
They ask,

if the house burns down
with everyone in it,
    which one of us gets to be the one who

survives & leaves?

No one can tell what goes on in between the person you were and the person you become... There are no maps of the change. You just come out on the other side.

— Stephen King

not a burial / but an unearthing

ONE SUNDOWN IN SAN FRANCISCO
(A PRAISE)

that time we said fuck it
& decided to take a knife to the night

& carve our dreams into the sky
we caught the stars as they fell

as we coughed the sunset out
dancing midnight into the moon's rise

it was all blue-burst & burning
a magnetic marvel, we were

with all that howl in our skin–
with all that & glow in our bones–

the stars did squint
when they saw us coming

& that was when we didn't have a beginning or an end—
just a becoming

the way we watched our skin unravel at the seams
how we took the streets & hazed the city

in our happiness
every lamplight glittered with lightning bugs

the men kissed on corners
women's skirts pulled up with consent for each other's

lips to collarbone, thighs pressed between hips

we rolled a joint in the mission,
smoked it on a curb in the castro

the scent of piss laced with glitter littered the air,
but the fumes of bourbon in our flask

cut the stench & o how we laughed
& laughed about everything

back then
we watched our feet float from under us–

the entire world removed from gravity,
i said, *i'd give anything for a typewriter or a pen right now*

& you said,
i need six strings to strum these feelings i have out

& away we went
to see what kind of art

we could bleed out
the typewriter became a cracked knuckle chorus

with each strike of the keys
your guitar looked like an open throat

the sounds we made were as simple as water–
it was a 3 am cleansing

i couldn't tell if i was more high on art, or on the pot,
but that did not matter

an orange tree grew in your backyard
we watched the sunrise

through its branches
i picked an orange & thought the sun herself

was dripping down my fingers
o san francisco,

you once were haven for the outcast & the artist
the way you let the queer kids wear your halo–

a cradle for the cracked
just because you exist in a thousand pieces

does not make you broken
we are all here on earth for something

a praise to the night & to the early morning
for the stranger at the coffee shop

who took me in & how we made art from dusk to dawn
a praise to the becoming

a praise to one random night in a city years ago that said,
welcome. yes, you

are welcomed here
just the way you are

THE HARVEST

I am married to a woman
who prefers to pick up our dog's shit
with the same shovel
she uses to dig the tomato beds.

No more than ten paltry fruits
blossom during each harvest.
She holds each one tenderly,
like it is full of blood & heartbeat.

I try to see the miracle in them, too.
Suppress my mind from reminding
me that there is poo in the soil,
which is why nothing grows.

She says, *Let's make salsa!*
Her eyes lit like Christmas trees
even in the sweat of a Texas July.
It is in the kitchen when I think about reincarnation– birth,

as I watch the massacre
of jalapeños & onion & garlic & cilantro &
our tomatoes the size of pimples
all blended to smithereens.

Isn't it beautiful, she says,
eyes aglow at the creation we made together.

I think,
Is this how straight people make babies? As simple as salsa.

The taking of two different things & mashing them together
to make something else? Something anew & alive?

I say, *One day I will give you salsa.*
& she smiles– chip in mouth crunching out the words,
Babe, you shouldn't buy something we can make ourselves.

I half-smile & say, *you're right.*
Not wanting to admit that no matter how perfectly our bodies fit together
when I said I could give her the world—

I lied.

ENDLESSLY

I.
Each morning we uncoil our bodies
into the light of a new, precious day.
All the while, the world seems to be crumbling just outside our window–
barely out of reach.
There is a certain guilt I feel wanting to not return to life as it was before.
Simply anchor my mouth to yours—
taste you endlessly.

II.
Your body is all I long to bow to.
Such a simple praise, my hands
skirting your waist, your skin—
my favorite river. How I follow your hips
same as the tide follows the moon. Limitless lovers. Holy water.
I will go forever wherever you guide me.
Lead me to the place you long.
May we capsize in the glory of our own making.

III.

It is a type of sorrow that we cannot make a child in the simple way.

Two consenting bodies colliding as one.

The love of two people bringing to life something anew.

I do wonder sometimes what they would be like.

Would they have your hands?

Be marveled by birds as much as I?

IV.

If we cannot make a child

then let me follow the hymn of your breath to a new destination.

Get lost in the labyrinth of your body.

It is no bother that the world is shuttered when there is no place I'd rather be.

Even on my knees, I have everything I want

before me.

LOVE IN THE TIME OF CORONA

It was the time when they loved each other best, without hurry or excess
— Gabriel García Márquez

It is the slowness of the morning that I love best—
one without rush. Being able to watch the sun rise like a flag.
It is the leisured sip of coffee. The waking for no other reason
than you are alive.

Before the time of Corona, everything seemed so hurried.
You would wake in a frenzy & I would hurtle out the door.
A clutter of cars would congest the highways.
Everyone seemed so anxious to be going— going
& I always have been one to wonder as to where
& why so fast?

As goes life, I suppose—
bye & bye & bye.

We don't have much time here on earth, really.
Even if we do make it one hundred years.
It has always been the greatest existential crisis—
trying to figure out what to make of it.
The one life you have.

What do I say, exactly, about love
in a time such as this other than it is a blessing.
Our bodies—
such temporary temples
that I do not take for-granted.

How profound it is to exist
O to love & be loved— what a gift.

ANTHONY

Man of the cuisine & culture.
Globetrotter of fried gallbladder & chicken beak.
Blood bather— table setter of the marbled beef.
I must admit, I never watched your show
until after you died. Isn't that how legacy works?
Remember Van Gogh?
The story about how he never sold a painting in his lifetime
but now, how we cherish his sunflowers.
Covet his blue period. You & I both know
how some profiteer off another's sadness.
You made a tv show out of yours.
Who knew *Parts Unknown*
was the name you gave
your depression.
Tried to swallow it down like tripe.
Fish lung.
I saw your shoulders sink
each time you sat at the table in another person's country.
I try to drink it out of me, too.
When you look at your face you see White /
Man / American / Rich.
Heritage of the atomic bomb
& slavery.
You shared a meal with a man from Vietnam
who was permanently maimed by our mistake.
But Anthony, we don't have to guilt our bodies
with the wrongdoings of our fathers—
we just have to speak out against their ghosts.
Let them know they are not welcomed in the land of the living.
I hope there is good food where you are &
better company with an endless river of beer.
I doubt you ever believed in such a place called heaven—
so a toast to you resting in an abundance of happiness.
A swarm of laughter. Good wine under a shitty chandelier.

GONE

I think of the dead.

Remember the empty shells of hermit crabs

& wonder where their bodies went?

I think of the autumn leaves, fallen—
dead.

Fall, brown /
dead
to the earth &
dissolve into the ground.

I think of skin & how it sheds.

Tiny bits of ourselves scattered
wherever we have been.

How we leave dead things everywhere.

How dead things leave us everywhere.

How one moment we are
& in the other we are not.

How it comes a time when the ones we know
become the ones we knew.

It is a wonder, isn't it?
How fast the world spins
& how— even if it is briefly,
we hang on.

THE MAIMING OF GRIEF

Every time a loved one dies you lose something. Maybe it is an entire thumbnail,

or an eyebrow   that never grows back. In some cases it can

even be a nose, or an ear   that disappears. It depends on the

relationship you had   with   the deceased.

The stronger the bond   the larger the missing   part of

the body   becomes.

I've heard of mothers who've given birth to a dead baby. — a still / born —   will

sometimes   lose their entire   heads.

At first it was a little strange,

people walking around   with missing parts,

but eventually everyone got used to it.

The wounding   of people   couldn't be easily placed.

No one knew if the cause of loss   was due to a car accident,   or

having no toes was because you were born without them. Now

everyone   wonders who you lost.   A

grandmother?   A   child?   A

father?   This maiming of grief would affect everything.   If a dog lost its

owner, would it   lose   a leg?   If a child lost their parents

maybe their eyes   would

disappear.   If you had all anatomy

intact   you walked whole, but with an   insurmountable fear of one day

waking up   fragmented,   like everyone

around you.   There were rumors that the loved

one   gone   was the culprit who took a

part of   your body

with them.   No one was angry by this.

Most were proud,   honored to have a part of them   live

with the one they loved,   the ones no longer

here.   Once there was a father who lost

his   entire family

in a wildfire.

He awoke one mourning

with no skin

not because of the flames

but because his

wife

still wanted to hold   on   to   a part of

him

& his

children still needed

the soft shape of their   dad.

I'D WAR FOR YOU

You tell me the story of how our skin is made of salt

      of how we were children of the sea

            before we were anything else

             you whisper me close & tell me to taste you

      your hair is a soft collapse; a tangle of eels

I breathe you in until my body feels buoyant & full

      of mist

      two capsized ships— we are

             our bodies; such beautiful wreckage

splayed across the ocean of our bed

      my hands follow the current of your skin

red fruit—

      open & wet,

             the water that makes us ripple

the salt of our bodies

      that connects us to the sea.

No wonder men fight wars over women.

I cannot fathom a war fought for anything less.

THE SUN IS A SHE

Today I squinted so hard
into the face of the Texas sun

I thought I had blistered my eyeballs.
I wanted to stare at the magnitude of her giving flame—

to be in awe of such a honeycomb in the sky.
The sun has always been a she to me.

Nothing makes you sweat quite like a woman.
A perfect sphere in our solar system—

she is both revered &
feared.

When I read how 1 million earths could
fit inside her hips I thought how wise she

was to keep us at such a distance.
What science says is that eventually the sun will consume the earth.

As I am writing this,
it is 165 degrees somewhere in Iran &

118 degrees in Austin, Texas.
I think she is getting closer.

I imagine it must be a terrible kind of lonesome to burn
everything you touch.

Is this how the woman is always blamed for the burden?
It isn't the sun's fault we are made of paper;

that we are not invincible against the torch of her smile—
the blister of her perfect skin.

BLOOM

When my PawPaw died my mom made me
come with her to visit his grave.

I never really knew the man,
but what I remember was noticing a flower
growing from his resting place.
I thought, *How beautiful — how strange,*
to find something blooming from his decay.

My mother was the one who taught me how to pray.
I was never really good at it & I realized why,
many years later, after reading Alice Walker say,
Any god I ever felt in church I brought in with me.

I see now why I've always felt holiness everywhere—
even in the places I'd least expect it.

I've seen it in the thunderstorm & the earthworm.
In the bullet that protects & the one that didn't.
How easy the seesaw of life shifts.

I've seen more hate spewed from people's Bibles
than I have from people's guns,

but the earth still spins
even though she has every excuse not to.

& the sun still spits its light even in the darkest shadows.
A bruise can come from the ugliest place,
but it still can be as gorgeous as an orchid in bloom.

I often doubt there is a god,
but I have never questioned Holy.

Sometimes I wonder why it is easier for me
to cry at the sight of kindness than it is
to wail at the sight of hate.

A wise man once said,
If you feed your children with food earned from corruption, they will be corrupt.
If you feed your children with food earned from honesty, they will be honest.

From here on out I'm going to fill myself up
on nothing but turnips of truth,
ingesting all the integrity I can swallow
just so I can tell my future children that honor
is the sweetest fruit.

This world may be an odd place,
but I'm going to embrace my own oddity.
I'm going to sing myself loud & proud
even if it's not on time & out of tune.

Cut the mic if you'd like,
but you can't unwrite what
I have scrawled across this heart.

Sometimes I feel like I am an open casket—
something dead,

but not quite buried.
& that's enough to get me up & going

even if it is a slow morning
& I mean that in more ways than one.

I don't always know where these poems are going,
but I do know this—

My PawPaw once beat
my Nannan's jaw into dandelion dust.

He almost killed three men in one bar fight
with his own bare hands.

After that he fled to Canada without his family
& he hid there for twenty-one years.

Despite what he did
my Nannan never loved another man like that

& my mom never stopped calling him *Dad*.
I didn't want to go to his funeral

because I could never respect a man like that,
but my mother told me through her tears,

Does anyone really know where the good grows,
or where the bad lives?

Some days I don't know what the fuck that means
& other days it makes complete sense.

Maybe this world is one whirling mess—
some broken-toe ballerina who can't stop dancing,

even if it hurts—
it would hurt even more not to spin.

We may all be hurling toward the edge of the cliff,
but no bird is born knowing it will fly—

it just does once it's tossed from its nest.
We might be an odd kind,

but I cannot believe that we are incapable of kindness.
This skin is all I've got

even if sometimes I don't like it.
This planet is the only home I know

even if I don't understand it.
My mother is right,

I do not know for certain where
the good grows or bad lives,

but I do know my heart.

This heart is an unstoppable engine
made of honey & pulp,
houses love in each chamber.

It never stops—
it just keeps going.

Every thump a billion blossoms bursting.

When the entire world seems to be withering
the clump of petals in my chest
is a reminder not to bleed,
but bloom.

Maybe it's animalness that will make the world right again: the wisdom of elephants, the enthusiasm of canines, the grace of snakes, the mildness of anteaters.

— Carol Emshwiller

What must the animals / make of us?

MISSISSIPPI RIVER (AN ALLEGORY)

In the year of the *Tie Snake*
the ground broke like a mouth–
jaw a'danglin in such a way
no doctor knew how to stitch it back.

1811 & 1812 were strange years
for that River.

Ain't nobody seen water try to walk away from itself.

The way it rose up like a clap
& completely snapped itself in half.

Made the white cowboys think biblically
while unpacking their belongings
& loading their guns,

but the Muscogees' knew the spirituality of ghosts.

They knew water don't turn on itself like that
unless there's gunna be a hauntin'.

The day the Mississippi River became a runaway
the fish all drowned.

The Muscogees saw the symbolism in the dead
creatures that they held in their hands,
so they bowed their heads & sang their hymns
to honor even the god of small things.

But the white man didn't understand.
They laughed at the Muscogees' reverence of creation–
called them ignorant
as they loaded their muskets & started shooting at the water
& anything & anyone around it–

what the white man has never learned is
that strength or god or bravery isn't found in a gun.

What the white man doesn't understand about the white man
is that he is & always has been the most dangerous one.

When the white men came to conquer
something that should have never been owned,
the River tried to drown itself—

dragged its wrists on its own rugged bottom.
There is a reason why the Mississippi still bleeds muddy–
why only weeping willows grow on her banks.

Why tornadoes travel through her towns
trying to take back what was stolen &
spit it back out.

The Muscogees fought as best they could,
but the weakest bullet will always win
over the strongest fist.

The victors will redefine savagery
& deny everyone else the pen.

What they will tell you is that the River ran backwards
due to a small earthquake—

but if you read between the margins what actually happened was this:

When the white man cupped his hands in the River for the first time
to wash his face clean, the River felt a chill so disturbing
that it actually grew legs   & ran.

WHAT OF THE HUMANS?

You think of every lightning bug you have ever held captive.
   The hermit crabs you didn't mean to starve—
      but did.

How you watched your childhood neighbor
   bash the brains out of living frogs
      against the wall.

How you have seen
   police do the same—
      but to people.

You think about every time
   you hit the dog
      & how the dog came back each time.

You remember in biology class
   how your body caved with
      an unexpected sadness

when you learned what we call the ravens— *an unkindness*.
How we describe a group of crows— *a murder*.

What must the animals call us?
An unhappiness of humans?

When they watch us war with one another
do we become a *hostility of humans?*

Do they warn each other when they see us
& howl, *a harmful of humans are approaching*?

I don't know why we ever anointed
ourselves with the word *humane.*

I think the animals have always seen us for who we are—
a hurting of humans.

They say,
Look— O how terribly wounded they all are.

TO THE SELF-DISTANCING PROTESTERS

I forgive them their unhappiness, I forgive them... But I don't forgive them for turning their faces away, for taking off their veils and dancing for death— Mary Oliver

You can call it what you wish—
Freedom.
Liberty.
Hoax.

The same as you did—
Parkland.
Orlando.
Sandy Hook.

But the fact is hospitals were filled.
There were parents / teachers / lovers / doctors
who never made it / home.

Children who received a burial
instead of a birthday.

There were those who died alone.

If I weren't so tired—
so confused—
so routinely disappointed—
I would be apoplectic with rage
as I have been
time & time & time again,
but not today.
Today my heart just breaks.
It breaks for the healthcare workers risking their lives

so that you can have your freedom.
It breaks for those on ventilators fighting for breath
as you use yours to shout propaganda
all while calling it patriotism.

It breaks for your total disregard for anyone
other than yourselves.
It breaks that you don't know the difference
between personal inconvenience
& the wellbeing or health
of someone else.
& perhaps that is the saddest part.
That you do know the difference,
but could care less.

I wish you cared about discrimination
as much as you care about getting a haircut.
I wish you cared about women's rights to their bodies
as much as you care about the rights to your guns.
Don't lecture me about the importance of freedom, liberty.
Where were you when I was fighting for my right to marry
the woman I love?
Where were you
when Eric Garner fought
for the essentialness of air?
You can have your freedom, your liberty
as long as everyone who is different than you can have theirs, too.

You can have your hoax
as long as it doesn't bring detriment
to others.

You can even have your anger—
but you cannot have mine.

That you have enough of.
So instead I wish you compassion,
the forgiveness of Christ.

If you one day make it to heaven
I hope the Lord has mercy, as I am afraid,

I would not.

JUST BECAUSE YOU DON'T SEE THE WONDER, DOESN'T MEAN THAT IT ISN'T THERE

the world is aflame
yet the sky tastes of honeydew.
tumbleweeds kick
toward the clouds. blue
is the warmest memory
you have ever had. your mother is an echo
in every forest. your father is a coat
in the closet you forget was still there
until it is cold & necessary to put on.
the rivers are flowing with honey
hot as molten. the air is thick with
cinnamon & tea. there are oranges
at your feet. come children, come.
play at the end of the earth.
leave the adults to their fear.
use the knives to cut the apples
into pieces to share aplenty. let every
wolf lick your face clean. offer
sugar cubes out of the palms of your
hands. run with the stallions in the endless field.
marvel at the murder of crows so alive
in the air. reach your hands out & up.
may each rain drop feel like a persimmon seed,
mouth open for the stillness of water.
thunder is a sound made when a flower blooms–
in this moment of the end you are

not running away,

but running *to*. your legs–

a marching band of hummingbirds

your chest— a stadium filled

with daffodils.

o children, come.

do you know that the moon is in your mouth?

speak stars into the darkness

fill this land with light

remind us how holy the dirt is

show us the miracle of sand

squeeze it until it slips through

your fingers like ants letting us see all that we cannot hold.

even you one day will be gone;

but not now. you are a thousand

lanterns glowing eternally

showing us what journey we all

had, once upon a time, in these

old bodies of chalky bones.

Little hymnal,

take every hand you can hold

& lead us to the ocean.

you don't have to say a word

your smile is a lit match

a pool of wonder

teach us just by being

remind us that the world is wide

enough—it always has been—

to hold everyone

if we let it.

ON WHY I DIDN'T OWN A SMARTPHONE UNTIL THE YEAR 2018

Because my flip-phone went kaput.
When I plugged it into the socket next to the microwave
The damn thing exploded like a hand grenade.

My body felt like an odd shaped specimen in the Sprint Store.
Everything blinked, but nothing could wink.
I found it sad.

The man who tried to sell me the iPhone was nice.
When I told him I worried about the bees—
he laughed.

He had no idea what I was talking about.
I gave a tired grin. I didn't want to explain to the kind man
about how 3 billion tons of electronic waste

end up in landfills that neither of us will ever see.
Show him images of suicide nets on the iPhone
he held in his hands explaining to me about widgets & apps.

I bought a Google phone instead
as if that is any better,
but I tell myself it is.

//

I walk in the grocery store &
tell myself that the price of these bananas
are good prices; fair prices—

even though I know about the banana trade.
I briefly reconsider. *Maybe I should buy organic instead?*
But they are .55¢ a bundle & some silly voice is telling me

that is too expensive when I know a banana farmer will work
8 hours a day in the smoldering heat
just to make $150 a month.

All I want is to go home & make a smoothie
even though I know the banana farmer
can't afford his own fruit.

//

When I lived in Costa Rica all I drank was instant coffee.
Andrés told me it is because my country bought
all of their best beans.

I forget in convenient spaces how I can afford so much.

//

I haven't owned a car since 2006.
I haven't eaten an animal
since 2009.

I say it is for noble reasons.

I don't want to contribute to greenhouse gas emissions.
I don't like the taste of sob or flesh in my mouth.
To be a knuckle in the fist

that continues to batter
the earth's skin
blue.

//

Do you find it ironic that every time we connect on our cellphones
a bee becomes disoriented & dies?
Research says that the frequency of our calls

causes bees to flee their hives.
That every time we figure out where we are on a map
a bee forgets its own home.

Knowing what I know now
I don't know why I still eat bananas
& not cows.

Why I still answer the phone when my mother calls
knowing that it could cause the death of something else.
Every day I wake up with the grand ambition of wanting to be better,

& every night I fall asleep wondering if I was.
Most days I ask myself whether to stay,
or run?

What I hate most about this smartphone
is that it is always trying to remind me where I am
when all I want, sometimes, is to simply forget.

MATING RITUALS

Did you know that when a male honey bee climaxes during sex, his testicles explode & he dies? Once the male Antechinus reaches puberty he will adventure on a two-week, non-stop, 14 hours a day sex session. These little marsupials literally fuck themselves to death. They don't eat, drink, or sleep, which then destroys their immune system to the point their fur falls off, they bleed internally, & become riddled with gangrene. Once they have reached such a decrepit state, the females, unsurprisingly, try to hide from them. & last, but not least, is the Bachelor Midge. A small fly who gets his blood sucked during intercourse & then in one interesting climatic finale, the female breaks his penis off, spiraling him to his final doom.

If you look to the animals, the females are often the ones with the power. How they can be both the creators & the destroyers. It makes me wonder that when man sought to make his own kingdom he feared the females the most— witnessed how nothing is subservient in the wild— watched aghast at how easy it is for a praying mantis to bite off the head of her suitor mid coitus. Stared in horror how a woman can bleed for seven days & not die. Man has always grappled with the fact that if he cannot control himself then he must control something or someone else & that makes him the weakest species of them all.

TAHLEQUAH

Tahlequah (also known as J35) was an endangered orca whale who gave birth to a daughter, who died 30 minutes later. She carried her dead daughter for over 17 days in an apparent show of grief.

I

Tahlequah is a Cherokee word meaning, *just two.*
& for 17 months & 17 days it was
just you & your daughter, Tali—
the two of you.

Your daughter was born
off the coast of Victoria. Not a stillborn
or a miscarriage, but alive—so alive,
if only for a moment.

II

For 17 days
& 1,000 miles you carried your daughter—
a dead thing, in your mouth.

O Tahlequah
is there another stage of grief for that?

What was heavier?
Trying to carry her,
or letting her go?

What must it feel like so weightless in water,
but still swimming in the weightfullness of loss?

In what moment did your heart fissure,
or did it just dissolve?

How mammoth can the emptiness of a whale be?

III

Time doesn't pass by us—
it goes through us.

It morphs everyone & everything—
has the power to change our bodies
& what's inside them.

Time took from you, Tahlequah,
but in the summer of 2020,
when the whole world was shut down—
when the planes weren't flying & the ships
weren't sailing, when the water finally
quietened from our noise, when we left
the fish alone & they multiplied
in abundance—it was then
you gave birth to another.

A son named,
Phoenix.

A happy, precocious calf—
healthy & thriving, the three of you
somewhere in the San Juan Islands,
swimming through the seasons
with you still holding the small shadow
of your daughter

because none of us ever let go completely—

everything rises in the end.

STAGES OF GRIEF, IN NO PARTICULAR ORDER

~

You hang up the phone & continue chopping the garlic. You don't notice that you've   minced everything in sight, including your own left hand. You heat the skillet with

olive oil. You put the onions & bell peppers & mushrooms in; pieces of skin mixed in   t h e mass. You don't even remember what you are cooking, but you continue on as if you

do. The skillet sizzles into a burn. Every smoke detector in the neighborhood goes off. *The   world has never stopped melting,* you think, as you watch the onions turn translucent— don't even notice the sound of the buzzing or the tears running down your face. Dinner is   ready. You spoon what you have made over rice. You eat & realize you have left something   out, but there is no one left to call now to figure out what it is.

~~

In a one arm swoop you push everything off the kitchen table. You break every plate in the   house. The dog licks the floor clean as a bone. You rush to the bathroom, turn on the cold water, jump in the shower with all your clothes, don't even bother unlacing your shoes—   just   shiver   in   your sweater as the water runs down your face— submerge—& hold your

breath for as long as you can.

~ ~ ~

Your eyes are swelled red
roses. When you touch your face
all you feel are thorns.

~ ~ ~ ~

It is simpler than you think, dear reader. It happens just like it does in all the movies & all   the books. Grief comes with all its shapes & shadows. It will be polite, knock on the door, tip its hat in an announcement it is here. If you lock it out, it will camp in the backyard, hide in the neighbor's tree. There will come a time when you finally say, *Okay.*

Come on in Grief. Let me make us a cup of tea. It'll oblige & you'll talk & cry & laugh & punch   & talk until there is nothing left to say or cry or laugh or punch or talk about anymore. At the end you'll take the dirty cups to the sink & escort Grief to the door, but it won't leave. It never does.

~ ~ ~ ~ ~

You wake up one morning, as you've done your entire life, but notice for the first time in your existence that the sky is everywhere. That no matter where we are on the planet, when we look up, we all see the same thing—space. Sure the clouds may be different in Melbourne & the sun could be blinding in Budapest & the stars could be out in Marfa, but here we are— wherever we are, underneath it all. Something about that makes you feel not so lonely— finding some sort of connectedness in the yonder above us. Certainly, you are still sad, & you have come to the understanding that a part of you always will be, but when you look up you'll know that what you see, they saw, too, & that, in a way, makes them last forever. Just like the sky— whoever it is, they are everywhere now, with you.

BROTHERLY LOVE

In order for us all to be together, for now we must remain apart
— Paramount Theatre, Austin, TX
We are all just walking each other home — Ram Dass

At the grocery store / we bandana our faces / & stand six feet apart /
waiting for each cart / to get sanitized / so we can quest /
through the aisles / searching / for non-perishables–
I like to think / it has much less to do with fear /
& more to do with care / concern / for one another /

the cashier is a kid / & I worry about her hands /
the way a mother must worry / the first time her child drives away /
to a new city / knowing no one /

I want us all to live /
to see another horizon / another blue, blue morning
noisy with birds / & / the people we love /
if I live long enough / to tell the tale of this time /

I want to say that we were tender / to each other / back then
that we saw / *really saw* / for the first time / how essential we all are /
that we remembered / how intrinsically connected / we always have been /
how our hands spread everything / both pleasure & pandemic /
how they can build / as easily as they can / break /
if I live long enough / to tell the tale of this time /

I want to say that we chose mercy / & yes / uncertainty did cloud the air /
people lost jobs / businesses went bankrupt / bars & restaurants & schools were closed
/
mortgages & rents unpaid / many went hungry, & yes–
/ many did die /

it was an unprecedented time / but despite the despair /
we still waved to our neighbors / we walked the dog /
we found ways to connect with each other again /
we marched / & rallied / & protested / & made art &
read books / & listened to whole albums / from beginning to end &
remembered / how important it is to reconnect / with family & friends /
even the schools continued / to provide free meals / although the doors /
were shuttered /

every medical professional was a knight / dressed in not the right armor/
but how gallantly they led the fight anyway / how they showed up same as soldiers /
& how we heralded them as such /
we rambled on rooftops / we kept quiet & / fell asleep to the soft sounds /
of the rumbling earth /
we paid attention to each other for once—
for once — saw how simple / fragile
/ we all really are.

What are you doing o living creature in this moment of history?

I hope it is wild / & full / of gracious / magical things /
when we meet again / I hope to hold your hand /
dear brother / I want to thank you / for walking me home.

Saudade is a Portuguese word that signifies a longing for something, someone that once was that will never be again. But it is not a sadness, rather a sorrowed gratitude, knowing that at least for a moment, you got to share a part of this existence with something, someone who gave you an irreplaceable, irrevocable joy.

Everything rises / in the end

SUNRISE IN SANTA FE

this morning I mistook the sky
for a tangerine
opened my mouth wide
as an apple
a river of ravens flew from
my throat
the entire earth spun like a jazz record
& for a moment
i forgot that blue was a sad color
& for a moment
i forgot all time & space & memory
i just stared at the miracle of all
that has always been
right here–

before us

IEMANJA

The memory of you appears, randomly,
many years later,
& just like that–

my head becomes a honeycomb
covered in bees.

The thought of you
& I, eight years prior,
that one autumn when we were
but twenty-three &

moved through the world untethered & unbothered,
when this city was more town than empire
how we weaved our way through our youth

like one dazzling swarm.

Your name,
Empress of the Ocean; Survivor of Shipwreck
& I am still trying to swim out from under you.

The girl who hand rolled cigarettes while walking in the rain
& dared me to fuck her under the stairwell on the Drag.
The girl who gave me my first pair of men's boxer briefs

because she saw how much weight the women's were to wear.
The girl who made me feel both beautiful & handsome
for the first time— in one breath.

Here I am.
Southampton, MA—
your alma mater.

I have sat parked on the side of the road
for the past forty-five minutes
staring into the abyss & writing this down

because the fog of your breath covers the entire city.
I cannot see a thing—
                                        not even your face.

METAMORPHOSIS

I languish for you . . . my sentiments for you are those of a woman.
— *Hans Christian Andersen to Edvard Collin*

I didn't mean to
      fall for woodsmoke
to prefer the taste
      of whiskey
off your tongue
      instead of
straight
      from the bottle
I don't know why
      my hands are petals
& not corduroy
      when I dream
it is of you
      a body of birch
your hair
   a mad tangle of moss
      I reach for you there &
when we touch I wake
      to nothing
          even my skin
             is gone

IF I COULD LOVE YOU THE WAY YOU LOVE ME, I WOULD.

I found myself unable to respond to this love, and this caused the author much suffering. — Edvard Collin on his relationship with Hans Christian Andersen

Peculiar.

The way you look at me.

Even more peculiar that I allow it.

That I actually enjoy it.

The way your eyes are two perfect dusk-

blue worlds &

I am the sun of them.

Sometimes you look as if you are on fire,

but confused by the flame.

I offer my hand

cool as water

on your back &

evaporate — I

disappear.

ODE TO ORGASM

uncontrollable throttle / hot air balloon

to outer space / every head

a tulip / your wet /

the milky way / moonjuice /

all stars turn into / tambourines

a city of cars crash / into an infinity /

of butterflies / your lover's mouth /

a lighthouse / luminescence /

when she opens /

ripple on water / soft

as a whisper / the way the ocean

spills / froth on the shore /

your hands / the gentlest hum /

my mouth open /

to your anthem

a song is a song is a song–

but yours a symphony

I hope to never stop singing.

WHAT MADE YOU SMILE TODAY?

I am aimlessly scrolling through my TikTok,
a bad habit I've been trying to quit,
when I come across a post that asks a simple question —
What made you smile today?

We are on who knows what day of self-isolation.
Twenty-two million people have now filed for unemployment,
businesses have been boarded, campuses closed,
hospitals still under-equipped, overcrowded—

yet here we are still finding reasons to smile.

Still bearing the whites of our teeth like the only lamplight
that will get us through this darkness.

It is its own kind of resilience
to make laughter your lifeboat.

To still dimple your way out of the desolate.

Reading reasons why strangers smiled
reminded me that it is always the simple things
that keeps us alive.

Someone posted about being mesmerized by the sunrise
& I thought, *O God, since when did we forget to look up?*

Another shared a photo of a field of flowers
& I thought, *O God, since when did we forget to look down?*

The flowers make me smile
knowing that they never give up.

The sun makes me smile knowing
that it never stops rising.

How they are both the gentlest reminders
that even when the entire world feels like it is wilting
there are still things that refuse
to do anything other than
blossom & rise.

QUARANTINE

the birds are whom i envy.
cawing & preening, the way they
zoom unfettered, an unfurling of feathers
across a sky that was once too clouded with noise.

i watch dazzled by the birds as they soar in an uncluttered blue
while we below are told to shelter in place.
& i, for once, am okay with the stillness.
the stopped cars & hushed streets.
the quiet comfort in knowing that we are all paused–
at least for a moment.

as long as the animals are allowed to dance
& the flowers have room to burst with their wild colors
& the bees can roam the quiet earth

i'll sit still, still, still.

i want to learn from the animals what to do in chaos, crisis.
what better creatures to learn survival from
than those who have survived time
& time again.

i want grace like that. i want to forgive like the trees.
to be as boundless as a bird. to know that when
i jump, the sky will go with me–
that i can land anywhere.

QUEER: A NOUN, AN ADJECTIVE,
A PLACE SOME CALL HOME

Adolescence was complicated for me.
How I looked one way, but felt another–
like a perfect painting
hung in the wrong hallway.

I was more interested in pick-up basketball games
than dress-up or slumber parties--
I preferred beating up boys instead of sleeping with them.

For a long time I wore tomboy
like a jersey nobody questioned.

I was twenty years old when I left Mississippi
with no direction to go other than
anywhere but here.

I felt like a unicorn in headlights the first time I made eye contact
with a queer presenting human in person.
They had a septum piercing & full arm sleeves.

When they asked what kind of creamer I used in my coffee
I almost squealed, *Glitter!*
Thinking that was the code word for,
I'm queer, too!

What that person doesn't know is that they showed me just by being
that you can claim your own skin, too.

Growing up gay in a small town you imagine the big city
to be your mecca.

Daydream about a destination
that sees you for everything you are
instead of everything you are not.

Identity should have never been something
you were taught to hide in the closet.

Shame is the worst kind of ghost,
but you don't have to let it be your haunting.

Use your love like a lightsaber.
May it be so blinding that it illuminates others out of the dark.
Show how heroic it is to live your one, true authentic self.
Know that there is inherent worth in your wondrous existence.

Little miracle,
queer kid from a town that can't seem to welcome your open heart.

Family isn't always the blood you are born from—
sometimes it is who you would rather bleed for.

There is a tribe of people just like you
all orbiting this wild, queer world together.

May we collide in the center—
a dazzling of curious confetti,
what we leave in our wake—
a chorus of color,
a litany of rainbows
across every place who tried to keep us
in the shadows.

Little lantern,
I see you. I see you.

What a gift—
your perfect light.
O how you glow.

A POEM FOR WHEN YOU NEED TO BE REMINDED OF YOUR OWN ELECTRICITY

What if I told you there were sparks in your spine
& handed you a match to strike against your vertebrae?
Would you believe in your flicker then?

Don't you taste the lamplight?
Have you forgotten the blowtorch that is tongue?

Your skin,
a satin stitched of stars. You,
the reason why the sun & moon
both compete for the light.

This poem is a benediction to you.

This world might be a labyrinth. A barrage of paths
with open doors & dead ends, but on days when darkness
seems like the only thing that exists remember
that in Spanish, *To give birth* is
Dar a luz meaning — *To give light*.

The spark never left your step, friend.
You are the glow that the moon comes to gawk at.

Yes, this world is a massive place
with a muddled sense of belonging,
but your bones
have always been yours.

Make the stars blush at the sight of your bright.
Tell the world you are here.
Sing your existence radiant & mighty.

Make us squint at the beam that is you.

Be an undeniable shine—
be so electric that this world
cannot help but be dazzled by you.

HOT AIR BALLOON

When there is food stuck in her teeth say something like,
You look exceptionally hot right now!
& when she asks, *Why?*

tell her you think that the black bean stuck
in-between her two front teeth
makes her look soooo...... *scrumptious.*

When she is grilling burgers in the backyard
come up behind her with all your sweet,
place your hands gently on her waist & ask,
Can I be your Hamburger Helper?

& when she says, *No, get out of here! Quit being so silly.*
Snatch the buns out of her hands & run away while yelling,
I'll be your Hamburglar then!

Make the one you love laugh unabashedly.
Apologize after every argument by holding your love so close
you both star in the same dream.

Be Bonnie & Clyde on their best day—
fugitive lovers.

Try your damnedest to escape your own bullshit.
Leave that to the therapist.

At the end of each day strive to bring
your best self to the table.
Show up with a bottle of Rosé,
but get so drunk on each other you forget all about it

in the fridge until next week.

Be patient & kind with the one you love.
Love panoramically.
Don't forget the moment because
you are so focused on the destination.

Sometimes you gotta pull over on a busy highway
in the middle of a rainstorm just
to pick the prettiest wildflower you have ever seen.
& when the cars honk at your crazy dance to their disdain,
yell with all the joy in your chest,
You don't understand because you aren't in love
the way I am, suuuuckaaas!

This is what being in love should do to you.
Make you feel like an astronaut
the way all gravity is lost when your love walks into the room.
Kiss her in a way that makes every lightning bug in the world—spark.

When your love feels lonely or sad,
don't tell her it will be okay.
Tell her you'll be a lighthouse.
That sometimes we all get lost at sea,
but the light at the shore will always be there—
that it never goes away.

Tell her you'll follow her everywhere…

//

except on a hot air balloon!
Because you are terribly afraid of heights.

& you also think sitting in a wicker
basket some 3,000 feet in the air held up with nothing
but a blowtorch is a tremendously stupid idea.

But if she *really* wants to go
you'll offer to pay for the ticket & take all the photos
& your love will respect your decision to stay on the ground

as you watch your love float away in that unsafe flying
flammable contraption because you promised
you would never hold her back–

so you won't.

//

promising your forever together is not about going
through the motions,
but sharing the conundrum,

experiencing the spectrum of all that is good &
sometimes what is hard & sad & angry
because life & marriage are a kaleidoscope.

It is a big, big house that is filled with secret bookshelves,
open doors, & closed windows that you attempt
to navigate the best way you can.

I'm sure you'll stump your toes on the furniture
from time to time, but you'll also come home
to find all the best ingredients in the pantry that you never realized you had,
make the perfect meal, & lick the plate clean & grateful together.

//

At the end of each day you must remember
to come to bed both open & honest.
Hearts full of fireworks & cotton candy for each other
like love is the best kind of carnival—
because it is.

As you fall asleep to the gentle breeze of your love's breath against your neck

& that is, perhaps, the closest thing to a happily ever after
any one of us could be blessed enough to get.

TO THE LIVING

My favorite thing to do as a kid was play pretend.
I got into so much trouble
for making shit up,
but what people didn't understand was that fiction
was the truth I lived in.

I'm thirty-three now &
all I really know is that I'm eleven states away
from a place I used to be
in a body I've now become &
I hope I never stop becoming.

I remember when the nurse asked me
while I laid in the hospital bed with a broken leg
if I thought it better to live
like you've got all the time in the world,
or rush through each day because you never know
when it could be taken away.
I said, *neither*.

I think that there will forever & always only be one you
with the right amount of time to be it,
so be it.

Even on your bad days know that you are lucky
because you've got enough tough in you to survive it.

Let the stars wink at the holy blink of you.

When the cynics come and try to cut your true
tell them there are too many possibilities

& doors in the world to stay locked
behind one.

Norman Cousins said it best,
The tragedy of life is not death–
but what we let die inside us while we live.

Never stop pretending.

Keep your mind in a constant state of bloom.

Look at the world & don't lose the wonder of it.

Remain in awe of the fact
that a blue whale has a heart the size of a Volkswagen van—
a heart so large you could build a home in it.

I want us all to have space to love like that.

To look up & not take the sky for granted.
To look down & be thankful for the ground.

But on the dark days– & there will be dark days –
when the phantoms come
to make you doubt if you ever belonged
you tell them ghosts that they cannot haunt a living thing–
& you, my friend,

you *are* living.

Hallelujah to the wonder &
glory of that.

SHOUTOUTS

A tremendous amount of gratitude to Write About Now for publishing this manuscript and taking me on this new journey with you. I couldn't imagine a better home. To Christopher "Rooster" Martinez, for seeing the vision of this work and helping me steer the ship to its correct destination. To my love, Katie, for giving me space to write– sometimes up to 8 hours a day– all while kindly reminding me that I have to eat. I love you. To Chibbi, your ability to do everything, all at once and perfectly, without fail or falter, is astounding and makes me want to work harder. To Amir Safi, your passion, vision, and commitment to spoken word is the lighthouse I always look to when I ever begin to question if anyone really cares about this artform. You remind me that the answer is a resounding, radiating– *Yes*. Thank you to my chosen family and blood family; I wouldn't be who I am if I didn't have both. To Maximus – my Great Dane shaped heart who passed away – I learned of joy and grief from you. An insurmountable amount of love to those who have supported me and followed my work over the years. Let's keep journeying together wherever these little poems take us. And lastly, I want to thank the animals. From the beginning, it is you who I have always looked to.

ABOUT THE AUTHOR

Lacey Roop is a genderqueer poet and performer. They perform their work nationwide at bookstores, campuses and festivals, including Austin Pride and the Desert Rocks Music Festival. They are a former Women of the World Poetry Slam finalist, and have been featured on PBS's Roadtrip Nation, reaching over 60 million households worldwide. A Mississippi native, they currently reside in Austin, TX with their spouse Katie and two incredibly large dogs (Artemis and Cassiopeia).

RECOMMENDED PLAYLIST

I like to write while listening to music, often more ambient or atmospheric genres. Below are recommended tracks to play alongside certain poems, as well as general music recommendations. I hope you enjoy the music as much as I enjoyed curating/sharing it with you.

Poem	Artist/Song
1. Queer: A Noun, An Adjective...	Grandbrothers/Alice
2. Bloom	Clint Mansell/Together We Live Forever
3. Just Because You Don't See the Wonder...	Peter Sandberg/Motion
4. Anthony	Nils Frahm/Some
5. Stages of Grief (in No Particular Order)	Ólafur Arnolds/20:17
6. Brotherly Love	Enzo/Red Dawn
7. What Made You Smile Today?	Dustin O'Halloran/Ed Funeral
8. To the Self-Distancing Protesters	Goldmund/Threnody
9. One Sundown in San Francisco (A Praise)	The Album Leaf/Seal Beach
10. Hot Air Balloon	The Album Leaf/The Light

To listen to the entire playlist follow me on Spotify @en_gallop13
"Writing Music" Playlist

OTHER TITLES BY LACEY ROOP

And Then Came the Flood, 2012 - Timber Mouse Publishing

OTHER TITLES BY
WRITE ABOUT NOW AUTHORS

Golden Brown Skin by S.C. Says
OTRO/PATRIA by M.R. "Chibbi" Orduña
Going Down Singing by Kevin Burke
They Rewrote Themselves Legendary by Ronnie K. Stephnes
Universe in the Key of Matryoshka by Ronnie K. Stephens
Rebel Hearts & Restless Ghosts by William James

WWW.WANPOETRY.COM | @WANPOETRY

CPSIA information can be obtained
at www.ICGtesting.com
Printed in the USA
LVHW011212270423
745399LV00005BA/521